The United States

Utah

<u>Paul Joseph</u>
ABDO & Daughters

visit us at
www.abdopub.com

Published by Abdo & Daughters, 4940 Viking Drive, Suite 622, Edina, Minnesota 55435.
Copyright © 1998 by Abdo Consulting Group, Inc., Pentagon Tower, P.O. Box 36036,
Minneapolis, Minnesota 55435 USA. International copyrights reserved in all countries.
No part of this book may be reproduced in any form without written permission from the
publisher.

Printed in the United States.

Cover and Interior Photo credits: Peter Arnold, Inc., SuperStock, Archive

Edited by Lori Kinstad Pupeza
Contributing editor Brooke Henderson
Special thanks to our Checkerboard Kids—Tyler Wagner, Aisha Baker, Priscilla Cáceres

All statistics taken from the 1990 census; The Rand McNally Discovery Atlas of The
United States.

Library of Congress Cataloging-in-Publication Data

Joseph, Paul, 1970-
    Utah / Paul Joseph.
    p. cm.
    Includes index.
    Summary: Surveys the people, geography, and history of this western state.
    ISBN 1-56239-890-3
    1. Utah--Juvenile literature. [1. Utah.] I. Title.
    F826.3.J67   1998
    979.2--dc21   97-34111
                                     CIP
                                     AC

Contents

Welcome to Utah

The state of Utah is located in the western United States. It is **bordered** by six other states. Utah's southeastern corner borders on Arizona, New Mexico, and Colorado. This is the only point in the country where four states meet in one place.

Utah's land is very uneven. The state has high mountain ranges, long stretches of barren desert, deep canyons, and many river valleys.

The development of the state began on July 24, 1847, when a group of 148 **Mormons** made Utah their new home. By the end of the year many more people had moved to the state. At the time it was called the Provisional State of Deseret—which is from the Book of Mormon. The word *deseret* means "honeybee," which symbolizes hard work.

Because of the **Mormons'** hard work, the area developed very fast. Schools were set up, streets were laid, and farms were started. All of this was under the leadership of Brigham Young.

Today, Utah, which takes its name from the Ute **Native Americans,** attracts many visitors. The beautiful land, Great Salt Lake, and wonderful people make this one of the best states in the country.

The Great Salt Lake in Utah.

Fun Facts

UTAH

Capital and largest city
Salt Lake City (159,936 people)
Area
82,076 square miles
(212,576 sq km)
Population
1,727,784 people
Rank: 35th
Statehood
January 4, 1896
(45th state admitted)
Principal rivers
Colorado River
Green River
Highest point
Kings Peak;
13,528 feet (4,123 m)
Motto
Industry
Song
"Utah, We Love Thee"
Famous People
Maude Adams, John Moses
Browning, Philo Farnsworth,
The Osmond Family, Brigham
Young

State Flag

Sego Lily

California Gull

Blue Spruce

About Utah

The Beehive State

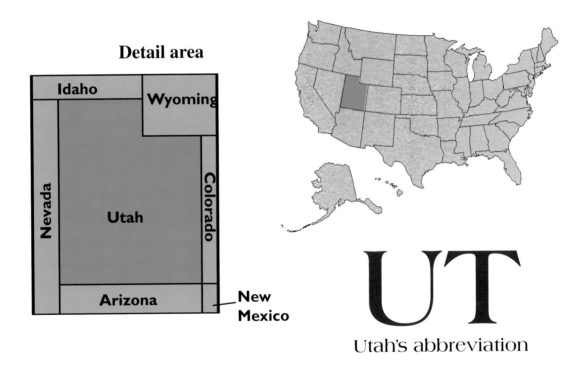

Borders: west (Nevada), north (Idaho, Wyoming), east (Colorado), south (Arizona)

Nature's Treasures

Utah has many wonderful treasures in its state. There are tall mountains, scenic lakes and rivers, beautiful national parks, thick forests, and valuable **minerals** under the ground.

The Great Salt Lake in Utah is the largest salt water lake in the western hemisphere. The water in this lake is even more salty than ocean water.

The mountains of the state offer excellent skiing, hiking, and scenic views. Zion, Bryce Canyon, Arches, Capitol Reef, and Canyonlands of Utah are some of the best national parks in the country.

More than a quarter of the state's land is forested. Some of the most common trees that grow in these forests are pine, spruce, and fir. Other parts of Utah, however, are desert where little grows except cactus.

Under the state's ground are **minerals**. Utah's minerals are among the richest in the western part of the country. Its most valuable minerals are copper, **petroleum**, coal, and uranium.

Not too many states offer as many different treasures as Utah. Because of the differences in the land and the treasures, people from all around the world visit this wonderful area.

The Colorado River running through the La Sal Mountains.

Beginnings

The first known people to live in Utah were **Native Americans**. The three major groups were the Ute, Paiute, and Shoshone.

In 1847, a group of 148 **Mormons** chose to live in an area that no one else wanted. The area was the canyon country of Utah, which offered little promise.

The development of Utah was very organized. The Mormons made lots of money on their land. In 1849, the Mormons organized the Provisional State of Deseret. They named the capital Salt Lake City. In the next 50 years, the state grew fast. Mormons and other settlers were coming from eastern states and Europe.

The Mormons wanted to make this new land a state. However, the United States government wouldn't allow it. The government didn't like their form of religion. In 1857,

President James Buchanan forced the **Mormon** leader, Brigham Young, to quit as **governor**. Attacks broke out between the Mormons and the United States. Finally, peace was made a year later.

The region's name was changed from the Provisional State of Deseret to Utah. In 1896, the United States government made Utah the 45th state.

A Mormon family in Utah in 1869.

B.C. to 1847

Early Land and People

 During the Ice Age, many thousands of years ago, Utah was covered by huge glaciers of ice. Many years later the ice began to melt and the uneven land of Utah began to form.

 The first known people to live in Utah were **Native Americans**. They were the Ute, Paiute, and Shoshone.

 1821: Mexico claims Utah.

 1824: Jim Bridger discovers the Great Salt Lake.

 1847: A group of 148 **Mormons** arrive in Utah.

Utah

B.C. to 1847

1850 to 1896

Territory to Statehood

 1850: The Territory of Utah is created. Salt Lake City is the capital. Brigham Young is the **governor**.

 1857: President James Buchanan removes Young from governor and the **Mormons** attack the United States troops. Peace is made in 1858.

 1863: **Mining** of silver and lead begins in Bingham Canyon.

 1896: Utah becomes the 45th state on January 4.

Utah

1850 to 1896

1919 to Now

Present Day Utah

1919: Zion National Park is created.

1964: Arizona's Glen Canyon Dam creates Utah's Lake Powell, the country's second largest man-made lake.

1990: Forest fires blaze in the northern part of the state, killing at least two people and burning more than 50 homes.

1995: Brigham Young's great-great-great grandson Steve, leads the NFL's San Francisco 49ers to a Super Bowl victory. Steve is also named the game's Most Valuable Player. He was born in Salt Lake City.

Utah

1919 to Now

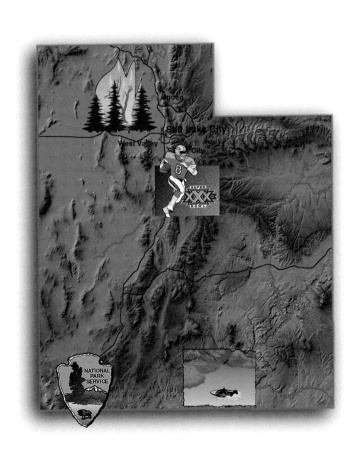

Utah's People

There are about 1.7 million people living in the state of Utah. It is the 35th most **populated** state in the country. The first known people to live in the state were **Native Americans**.

Today, many well-known people have made Utah home. The most famous person that lived in Utah is Brigham Young. He was the second president of the Mormon Church.

In 1847, Brigham led his **Mormon** followers all the way across the United States to settle near the Great Salt Lake in Utah. He became Utah's first **governor**. Brigham Young University (BYU) was named after this leader.

Brigham Young's great-great-great grandson, Steve Young, also lived in Utah. Steve Young is the All-Pro quarterback for the San Francisco 49ers. As a young boy he moved to Connecticut. He did, however, come back to star both in the classroom and on the football field at BYU.

Other famous people that lived in Utah are movie star and director Robert Redford; football player, actor, and sportscaster Merlin Olsen; and Willard Marriott, who started the chain of Marriott Hotels.

Robert Redford

Brigham Young

Steve Young

Splendid Cities

Utah has many splendid cities in its state. Only one city in the state has more than 100,000 people. Most cities in Utah are small in **population**, but they still have many things to do and see.

Utah's capital, Salt Lake City, was founded by the **Mormon** pioneers. The city has about 160,000 people living in it. Because of its historical sites, magnificent mountain setting, and the Great Salt Lake nearby, the city draws many visitors.

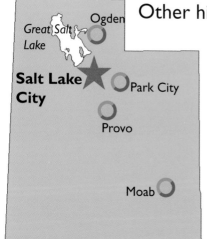

Other highlights of Salt Lake City are the University of Utah, the Mormon Temple and Tabernacle, and Sea Gull Monument.

Provo is located 40 miles south of Salt Lake City. It is a **manufacturing** city known for making computer software, electronics, steel, and clothing. Provo is best known for being the home to Brigham Young University. It is one of the largest private colleges in the country.

Park City has less than 5,000 people living in it. However, it is very well known and in the winter very crowded. It is one of the best ski **resorts** in the country. People come from all over the world to ski in Park City.

Other cities in Utah are West Valley City, Sandy City, Orem, Ogden, Layton, Bountiful, and Moab.

Salt Lake City, Utah

Utah's Land

Utah has some of the most beautiful and different land in the country. There are lakes, rivers, mountains, forests, canyons, and deserts. The state has three regions.

The Rocky Mountains region is an L-shaped area in the northeastern part of the state. This area is covered by mountains, rivers, and forests. Kings Peak, the highest point in the state, towers over the land.

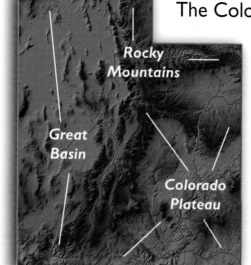

The Colorado Plateau region in southeastern Utah covers a big part of the state. This region is filled with colorful mesas, cliffs, and other highlands. It also has the deep gorges of the Green and Colorado River.

The Great Basin region reaches down through western Utah. It is a land of vast deserts, salt flats, and block mountains. The Great Salt Lake and the Great Salt Lake Desert are in this area.

The Great Basin has many rivers. It is also home to the lowest point in the state. At 2,180 feet (664 m), the lowest point in this state isn't very low!

Zion National Park

Utah at Play

Utah is a great place to play. There are so many different things to do and see in the state. People are attracted to Utah's beautiful land, mountains, the Great Salt Lake, national parks, and museums.

Utah attracts more than 10 million **tourists** each year. People are attracted to skiing **resorts** in Park City, Alta, and Snowbird. The incredible mountains in Utah offer some of the best skiing in the world.

Mountains tower all around the Great Salt Lake. Although people don't usually swim or boat in the lake, it is a very scenic area. There are fresh water lakes and rivers where people enjoy swimming, fishing, or boating.

People enjoy playing in the many state and national parks that Utah has. The state also has many national monuments and six national forests.

Inside, people enjoy the fine museums of the state, the many temples, and a basketball team. The NBA's Utah Jazz play in Salt Lake City.

Utah offers some of the best skiing in the world.

Utah at Work

The people of Utah must work to make money. There are many different kinds of jobs that people do in the state. With 10 million visitors every year, a lot of the people work in service jobs. Service is working in hotels, **resorts**, restaurants, and stores to name a few.

Other people work in the **manufacturing industry**. The manufacturing of cars and trucks ranks first in importance. People also package food, and work at factories that make stone, glass, and clay things.

Other people in the state are miners. The **mining** industry in Utah is a very large business. **Petroleum** is the most valuable **mineral**. Utah's Bingham Canyon supplies more than 10 percent of the nation's copper. Other minerals there are lead, gold, silver, zinc, coal, and iron ore.

Some people in Utah work on the 13,000 farms in Utah. Farmers grow **crops** like onions, potatoes, and fruits. The **grazing** area for animals has over one million cattle, sheep, and deer.

There are many different things to do and see in the state of Utah. Because of its natural beauty, people, land, mountains, and **resorts**, Utah is a great place to visit, live, work, and play.

Bingham Copper Pit Mine is the worlds largest pit of its kind.

Fun Facts

•Utah has more kids under ten than any other state. And kids living in Utah spend more years in school than in any other state.

•Utah is known as a very dry state. It doesn't get much rain because the Sierra Nevada, to the west of the state, robs the winds that creates rain and moisture. Parts of the Great Salt Lake Desert receive less than five inches (13 cm) of rain a year!

•In 1848, crickets were invading the state. They were all over and their chirping was very loud. Thankfully, sea gulls stopped this invasion by eating them.

•Grasshoppers also were invading the state and ruining the farmer's **crops**. In 1854, they too were put to a stop.

•Brigham Young is the most famous person ever to come from Utah. His great-great-great grandson, Steve Young, is an All-Pro NFL quarterback for the San Francisco 49ers.

Zion National Park, Utah.

Glossary

Border: neighboring states, countries, or waters.

Crops: what farmers grow on their farm to either eat or sell or both.

Explorers: people that are one of the first to discover and look over land.

Governor: the highest elected official in the state.

Graze: animals eating grass.

Industry: many different types of businesses.

Manufacture: to make things by machine in a factory.

Minerals: things found in the earth, such as rock, diamonds, or coal.

Mining: working underground to get minerals.

Mormons: the name of people that belong to a religious group known as the Church of Jesus Christ of Latter Day Saints. Mormons do not smoke cigarettes or drink alcohol. Many Mormons live in the state of Utah.

Native Americans: the first people who were born in and occupied North America.

Petroleum: also known as oil. An oily liquid that is obtained from wells drilled in the ground. It is used to make gasoline, fuel oils, and other products.

Population: the number of people living in a certain place.

Resort: a place to vacation that has fun things to do.

Tourism: a business that serves people who are traveling for pleasure, and visiting places of interest.

Internet Sites

Utah's Virtual Valley
http://www.itsnet.com/home/johnb/
Virtually everything you would want to know about Utah, from schools to sports.

Web Utah
http://www.webutah.com/fast.html
We have the largest collection of links to Utah Web sites available on the Internet (309 sites). We have tried to make searching as easy as possible through a variety of different formats. You can search by keyword, city, topic, or a combination of all of these.

These sites are subject to change. Go to your favorite search engine and type in Utah for more sites.

PASS IT ON

Tell Others Something Special About Your State
To educate readers around the country, pass on interesting tips, places to see, history, and little unknown facts about the state you live in. We want to hear from you!
To get posted on ABDO & Daughters website, E-mail us at "mystate@abdopub.com"

Index